Other Things to Do

by Mar
Illustrations

RAINBOW READING

It was lunchtime at Central School.
The children were outside playing.
The teachers were having lunch
in the staffroom.

There was a knock on the staffroom door.
"Excuse me.
Our ball's stuck on the roof again."
"That's the third time today!" said Mr James.
"I'm sorry
but it'll have to stay there until tomorrow.
Maybe then, you'll be more careful
how you play with it.
You can find other things to do today.
We need some peace."

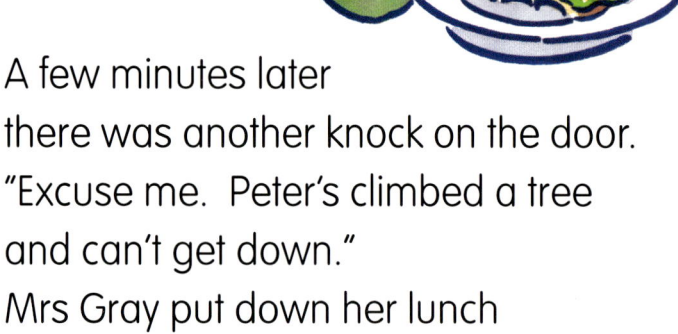

A few minutes later
there was another knock on the door.
"Excuse me. Peter's climbed a tree
and can't get down."
Mrs Gray put down her lunch
and went to help.

Mrs Smith got up to make a cup of tea.
She looked out the window.
"There are children fighting out there.
I'll have to go and stop them."

Mr Munro got up to wash his cup.
"I can see children playing in the garden.
We can't have that!"
He ran outside.

Not long after, there was another knock on the door.
"Excuse me. Our kite's tangled in the tree."
Mr Lambert went to help.

"I think we'd better get that ball down from the roof," said Mr James. "Maybe then, we'll get some peace."